CHASING ME DOWN

THE MESSAGE BEHIND THE MUSIC

JARED MILLER

Chasing Me Down: The Message Behind the Music
Copyright © 2018 by Jared Miller
All rights reserved

Published by RevMedia Publishing
PO Box 5172
Kingwood, TX 77325

ISBN 978-1-7324922-9-5
Printed in the United States of America

CONTENTS

CONTENTS

ACKNOWLEDGMENTS

To my wife Courtney, you are my best friend and the love of my life. You are a living example of God's love to our boys and me every day. Thank you for believing in me and this book. I love you and am thankful to be your husband.

Grayson and Owen, you boys are the joy of my life. I thank God for you every day. I'm so proud to be your dad!

To my family, Dennis, Mom, Jon, Paige, Robert and Wanda: thank you for your love and for supporting the dreams and calling God has on my life. Family is everything. I love each of you so much.

Pastor Frank Mazzapica, thank you for taking a chance on me thirteen years ago. Thank you for believing in me and trusting me to lead our wonderful New Covenant Church family in worship every week. It's a privilege and an honor.

NCC Family, so many of you have supported me on this project. The music and the message of this book would not be possible without your prayers, support and love. I am truly humbled and thankful.

Mark Townsend, thank you for your mentorship. Thank you for pouring into my life. Most of all, thank you for your friendship. You opened my eyes to opportunities that I never thought were possible. I am forever grateful.

Nick Cooper, one meeting with you changed my life forever. You are a gift to me and to the world.

Aimee Pierce Olmsted, thank you for taking the time to edit this book. You have been a huge encouragement to me in this endeavor.

Most importantly, thank you Jesus for chasing me down at the young age of 6. Thank you for giving me life and purpose. All that I am is because of You. I pray that this book brings You glory and blesses Your people.

FOREWORD

I love worship! Having been a musician and producer most of my life, I've had the opportunity to play a variety of genres and events. From jazz to funk cover bands, pop to worship, in living room concerts to stadiums and everything in between. I can honestly say my favorite scene is the worship scene. The tangible presence of God experienced with like hearted people is an epic treat that I love to be a part of.

This is a real honor for me to be a part of this book, as it was being a part of the project "Chasing Me Down". The book as well as the music is life changing when the revelations contained within start to burn within. The very title describes a very different view of God than is presented by religion. Religion encourages us to pursue God with all of our hearts, while the gospel of Jesus Christ as revealed by the Apostle Paul reveals that God has relentlessly pursued us and captured us with His love.

2 Corinthians 5:19 states:
> "...in Christ God was reconciling the world to himself,
> not counting their sins against them, and entrusting
> to us the message of reconciliation."

Notice who it is that God "doesn't count their sins against them"? Is it the christians? No - He chased down the entire world and demonstrated irrevocably that they are forgiven. As Jared mentions in the book the account of Jesus forgiving his murderers on the cross, I would ask - did He wait for them to jump through any hoops before he commanded forgiveness? Did they confess, believe, repent, rub beads together, pray the sinners prayer, or get baptized? No - God went ahead and reconciled the whole world to himself, making everything right at the cross. When was the last time you told a pre-believer that "God doesn't count your sins against you"? Maybe it's time the church begins to share the good news of what God knows to be true about all of humanity. After all - we've been given "the ministry of reconciliation". Paul goes on to state "be therefore reconciled to God". Note he did not say "become reconciled to God". That's not particularly good news when there are so many versions in religion of how we would go about doing that. The good news of the gospel is that God chased you down and fixed the problem from His perspective.

This explains why Colossians 3:11 declares that "Christ is all and in all", and Ephesians 4:6 declares that God the Father is in all as well. Peters vision in the book of Acts shows him that "he should call no man common or unclean". 2 Corinthians 5:16 - Paul echos Peters sentiment when he states "from now on we regard no man from a worldly point of view". Even John 1:9 states that Jesus "...was the true Light, which lights every man that cometh into the world."

Reconciliation is a very deep concept when applied to relationships. Think of a married couple that may have been separated or divorced. If they experience reconciliation, there is intimacy, oneness. Think of the word "atonement" in terms of "at-one-ment". Two people are now at one, with perfect union.

Ultimately the quality of our praise and worship is tied to the degree we acknowledge the divinity of all humanity. James reveals this in James 3:9,10:

With the tongue we praise our Lord and Father, and with
it we curse human beings, who have been made in God's
likeness. Out of the same mouth come praise and cursing.
My brothers and sisters, this should not be.

Jared outlines this beautifully in chapter 3 - "Characteristics of Lifters". Part 2 of that chapter details how we should honor all people. How can we do this when we see all manner of bad behavior in people? For starters - we can stop walking by sight. We walk by faith in what Jesus came and revealed about us - that we are forgiven regardless of how bad the sin is. After all, there is nothing more evil than deicide, and we know Jesus forgave that without hesitation.

This refreshing and biblical view on the goodness of God is currently exploding in the earth. As has often occurred in history, the worship leaders and musicians are leading the charge. Old mindsets are being broken off regarding the nature of God the Father. People are awakening to the reality that we have all been justified - just as if I'd never sinned - single handedly by one mans righteous act of obedience (Romans 5:18). We have been made righteous, perfect, and blameless by design (Gods image and likeness), rather than our performance or human effort. In fact - Paul reveals in Galatians 3 that human efforts aimed at improving our standing with God are "witchcraft".

It is this revelation of grace that "teaches us to say no to unrighteousness". For too long religion has given us laws and rules to keep to try and clean ourselves up. The gospel teaches us that we "all died with Christ" (2 Corinthians 5:14) and our sin nature was circumcised away (2 Corinthians 2:11). Thank God circumcision is a one time operation. There's nothing left to fix - either you are sinless and don't have a sin nature, or the cross was a sham. The more we awake to this reality - the more we act like it. The gospel approaches sin the opposite of religion - your sin nature was destroyed at the cross, so now act like it!

As you read the following pages - let the Spirit of God within you enlighten you to the reality that God the Father is a good God. He will never leave you or forsake you. I can say this based on more than just the revelation in scripture as well as the life of Jesus, I've lived it. Throughout my life, His goodness, mercy, blessings, bliss, righteousness, peace, and joy have been relentlessly CHASING ME DOWN.

-Mark Townsend

INTRODUCTION

It was the spring of 2017. I was in the middle of working on my solo worship project when my producer, Mark Townsend, and I began a conversation over lunch about the message of the gospel. From Pappasitos (arguably the best fajitas ever) to Starbucks, that conversation led to the songs that would eventually become the Chasing Me Down record.

I have sung and led worship for as long as I can remember, which is what I'm known for. However, I also have a passion to teach and create resources that will help people in their spiritual growth and take them to a higher level. My prayer is that what you read in the following pages will do just that: take you higher. Friends, with God there are no limits. Each day that you read this book, believe with faith that the Holy Spirit is stirring up the gifts of God inside you.

Howard Thurman asserted, "Don't ask what the world needs. Ask what makes you come alive, and go do it. Because what the world needs is people who have come alive." I pray that the Holy Spirit would cause your dreams and visions to come alive as you read this book.

The following pages are not stories behind the songs, but rather they're the message of the songs. At the end of each chapter you will find daily reflection questions to help you pause, think, and apply what you have read to your daily life. You will notice that there are six reflection questions, not seven. I have intentionally written only six questions: one question for each day, because the seventh day is meant to be a Sabbath and a time of rest. Let me encourage you not to rush through the questions but to use them as a daily devotional for your spiritual growth.

CHASING ME DOWN

Goodness all around
There is nowhere I could go
Where your love's not found
Surrounding my heart with yours

Your love broke through my
Walls when I saw
You were the one
Chasing me down
Was lost but now I'm found

I can feel your love, your love
All around me
Everywhere I go
I can feel you move, you move
All around me
You never stop, never stop
Chasing me down

You never fail
You won't give up on me
I have a joy
That is my strength
I have this hope
Christ in me

Words and Music: Jared Miller/Mark Townsend

"If you are 1000 steps from God, He will take 999 steps in your direction."

CHASING ME DOWN

Your beauty and love chase after me
Every day of my life -Psalm 23:6 (MSG)

As a kid growing up in church, my friends and I enjoyed nothing more than running around the sanctuary chasing each other until one of us was caught. The fun usually lasted until one of our parents eyed us down with "the look" and explained that running in the church building was not appropriate. Hey, we were kids and we were having fun. There was a thrill to being chased. The feeling of adrenaline kicked in, enabling us to go from 0 to 60 in no time just so we wouldn't be caught.

What comes to mind when you think of being chased? Does it scare you? Does it make you anxious? I'm the type of person who doesn't care too much for people looking over my shoulder, let alone following me. My impulse is to get away and be left alone as fast as possible. Can you relate?

For most of us, the issue with being chased or followed is due to a fear of the unknown. Who is this person, and why is he following me? Every thought imaginable runs through our heads like a flash of lightning and ends up leading us to the worst possible scenario. Fear has that effect on us. It paralyzes and debilitates our confidence. I've heard it said that fear is False Evidence Appearing Real. Fear is an illusion. Fear is a liar. What is on the other side of fear? Nothing! You mean I've been stressing out and worrying all this time in vain? Yes!

Fear of the unknown causes us to go into panic mode, because we realize that we are not in control. When it comes to our faith in God, maybe that's the point: not being in control. In order for us to relinquish control, we have to trust God. Building that trust takes time. Here is the good news. God created time, and He is not bound to the structure of time. He is patient with us. His love for humanity is so much greater than you or I could ever comprehend. God doesn't just love; He is love. God loves you, and He will never stop loving you. Nothing you could do or say could ever change that. Author Tim Keller was quoted proclaiming "The founders of every major religion said, 'I'll show you how to find God." Jesus said, "I am God who has come to find you."

One of history's most beloved chapters in the Bible is Psalm 23.

A Psalm of David
The Lord is my shepherd;
I shall not want.
He makes me to lie down in green pastures;
He leads me beside the still waters. He restores my soul;
He leads me in the paths of righteousness

For His name's sake.
Yea, though I walk through the valley of the shadow of death,
I will fear no evil;
For You are with me;
Your rod and Your staff, they comfort me.

You prepare a table before me in the presence of my enemies;
You anoint my head with oil;
My cup runs over.
Surely goodness and mercy shall follow me
All the days of my life;
And I will dwell in the house of the Lord
Forever.

Wow! You can't read Psalm 23 without feeling a sense of peace and confidence. Let's take a look at the promises God gives us through this psalm. In verses 1-3, God gives us provision and protection. I recently read a fascinating story by Dawn Carrillo that really depicts God's love and protection for his people. She writes, "Sheep can get their head caught in briers and die trying to get untangled. There are horrid little flies that like to torment sheep by laying eggs in their nostrils which turn into worms and drive the sheep to beat their head against a rock, sometimes to death. Their ears and eyes are also susceptible to tormenting insects. So the shepherd anoints their whole head with oil. Then there is peace. That oil forms a barrier of protection against the evil that tries to destroy the sheep." Do you have times of mental torment? Do the worrisome thoughts invade your mind over and over? Do you beat your head against a wall trying to stop them? Have you ever asked God to anoint your head with oil? He has an endless supply! His oil protects and makes it possible for you to fix your heart, mind, and eyes on Him today. There is peace in the valley! May our gracious Father anoint your head with oil today so that your cup overflows with blessings!

Our God is the Good Shepherd. He restores us and leads us in the way we should go. In order for God to lead us, we must be willing to follow Him. In order to follow Him we must trust Him, and that takes faith. The Omniscient, Omnipresent, and Omnipotent God of the universe does not force us to follow Him. He neither manipulates nor drives us as a taskmaster would. Instead, He invites us to follow Him to the greatest life we could ever imagine. Allow me to give a quick sidebar. We talk a lot about being driven in life. I understand the concept and the motivation behind the idea, however in Scripture, the only thing that Jesus ever drove were demonic spirits. Jesus leads His people. Jesus does not force us; He allows us.

Verses 4-5 get better. When I walk through the valley of the shadow of death, I will fear no evil for You are with me. What a promise! God is right beside you in the darkest moments of your life.

A shadow by definition is a dark area or shape produced by a body coming between rays of light and a surface. Remember this, you cannot have a shadow unless there is light. Jesus is the Light. He is the Light that shines in the darkness. John 1:4-5 says, "In Him was life, and the life was the light of men. And the light shines in the darkness, and the darkness did not comprehend it." Get excited! Even when you feel like you're going through a dark situation, there is light shining all around you.

Psalm 23:5 reads that God pours out so many blessings for us so that our enemies can see how good God really is. As if these promises aren't enough, it gets even better. It almost feels like these Scriptures are infomercials saying, "but wait, there's more!"

Pay close attention to verse 6: "Surely goodness and mercy shall follow me all the days of my life." Check out The Message translation of verse 6: "Your beauty and love chase after me every day of my life." God is saying, "My goodness and my mercy is chasing you down every day of your life, and there is nothing you can do to stop it." He pulled the God card. He didn't consult with you, and He didn't ask for your permission. He loves you with an undying, unconditional love that surpasses the thoughts and understanding of your mind.

You can trust Him. You don't have to be fearful of being caught. You can be free of fear today. Place your trust in the One who gave His life for you. As if giving His life for you wasn't enough, He has more to give. God has an endless supply of peace, joy, and love. Look at Ephesians 3:20-21: "God can do anything, you know—far more than you could ever imagine or guess or request in your wildest dreams! He does it not by pushing us around but by working within us, his Spirit deeply and gently within us" (MSG).

Like kids playing tag, God is saying to you, "Tag! You're it!" God's love for you has never stopped and it never will. Are you ready to receive all that God has in store for you? Stop fear dead in its tracks. Respond to God calling out to you. It is time to starve your fear and feed your faith. Believe that God is in control and that your life is in the palm of His hand. Feel the freedom that comes when you totally surrender your life to Him. You can trust Him. He will never fail you. If you are 1000 steps from God, He will take 999 steps in your direction. God's love is chasing you down. Can you feel it? In the next chapter, we will take a deeper look at God's love for us.

DAILY REFLECTION QUESTIONS

1. When have you experienced God's love at work in your life?
2. What are key moments where you have felt God's protection?
3. Can you think of a time when God's grace and mercy have chased you down?
4. How does it make you feel knowing that God is always with you?
5. What does it mean that God is working within us?
6. How has God's light strengthened you during dark times in your life?

LOVED BY YOU

This is a feeling I can't describe
I feel your love and I come alive
It's taking me over
I have no reason to feel afraid
I know you hear when I call your name
You are with me

And I have a hope
Your Spirit comes alive and overwhelms my soul

This is what it feels like / This is what it feels like
To be loved by You / To be loved by You

Like the rain crashing over me
It's coming in like a raging sea
I'm swept away by your love
Oh I know it goes on and on and on and on

And when I feel afraid
I trust that you're near me
If you feel far away
I know that you're inside of me
If I wonder away
You're right there waiting for me
Cause I walk by faith and not by sight
When night gets dark to you its daylight

This is what I'm made
Life is so much more
Now that I'm loved by you

Words and Music: Jared Miller/Isaiah Rangel/Mark Townsend

"The feeling that God values me and loves me causes me in return to do the same for others."

LOVED BY YOU

"The greatest thing that we can do is to help somebody
know that they're loved and capable of loving."
-Fred Rodgers (Mr. Rodgers)

I'd like to start this chapter by reading truths about God's love. Read them and see which statement sticks out to you:

God loves me.
God loves you.
God loves people I don't know.
God loves people I don't like.

If you are like me, that last statement struck a nerve. Loving those who have wronged me is not easy, but it is exactly what Scripture instructs us to do. Matthew 5:43-48 in The Message translation states, "You're familiar with the old written law, 'Love your friend,' and its unwritten companion, 'Hate your enemy.' I'm challenging that. I'm telling you to love your enemies. Let them bring out the best in you, not the worst. When someone gives you a hard time, respond with the energies of prayer, for then you are working out of your true selves, your God-created selves. This is what God does. He gives his best—the sun to warm and the rain to nourish—to everyone, regardless: the good and bad, the nice and nasty. If all you do is love the lovable, do you expect a bonus? Anybody can do that. If you simply say hello to those who greet you, do you expect a medal? Any run-of-the-mill sinner does that. In a word, what I'm saying is, grow up. You're kingdom subjects. Now live like it. Live out your God-created identity. Live generously and graciously toward others, the way God lives toward you."

We all desire to love and to be loved. That desire is universal and intrinsically placed in every soul. Luke 6:38 says, "Give, and you will receive. Your gift will return to you in full—pressed down, shaken together to make room for more, running over, and poured into your lap. The amount you give will determine the amount you get back."(NLT)

You can only give love if you have love. Truthfully it is not simply love that we crave, but rather it is unconditional love: the love that only God can give and has given to us all. God is able to give love because the Bible says that God is love (1 John 4:8).

GOD LOVES AND KNOWS THE REAL YOU

Psalm 139:1-4 describes how well God really knows us. "O Lord, you have examined my heart and know everything about me. You know when I sit down or stand up. You know my thoughts even when I'm far away. You see me when I travel and when I rest at home. You know everything I do. You know what I am going to say even before I say it, Lord" (NLT). Isn't it amazing that God loves us in spite of all of our flaws and mistakes?

GOD'S LOVE IS CLOSER TO YOU THAN YOU REALIZE

Pastor Carl Lentz asserted, "Proximity creates passion. Distance creates distortion. Whatever you're close to, you will be passionate about. Whatever you're far from, you will not care about." Psalm 139:7-8 describes it this way: "Where can I go from your Spirit? Where can I flee from your presence? If I go up to the heavens, you are there; if I make my bed in the depths, you are there" (NIV). God is always with us. This became extremely evident on December 9th, 2000.

I was actively involved in a youth internship program at Triumph Church in Nederland, Tx when my life changed forever. My cousin began banging on the door of the house where I was staying. He informed me that my Dad was in the intensive care unit due to a ruptured blood clot. We rushed to the hospital praying everything was ok. After the almost two hour drive, I ran to his room, but he was nowhere in sight. I asked the nurse where they had taken him. She began to inform me that he had deceased. Blindsided, caught off guard, in shock, you fill in the blank; In one moment, I experienced all of these emotions and more. I felt the weight of the world crashing down on me. Everything around me seemed to stop. On the outside, my world was crumbling. On the inside, God was holding me in His hands and wouldn't let me go. It was here where I felt God's peace and love in a way that I had never experienced before. My awareness of God's strength held a whole new meaning. What I thought would destroy me actually developed me. That was 18 years ago. There are some things that happen in our lives that we may never fully understand. One thing is for sure; "God is our refuge and strength, a very present help in trouble". Psalm 46:1 (NKJV) He is near to the broken-hearted. God is close. Closer than we realize.

GOD'S LOVE HAS ALWAYS BEEN AT WORK IN YOUR LIFE

Psalm 139:13-16: "Oh yes, you shaped me first inside, then out. You formed me in my mother's womb. I thank you, High God—you're breathtaking! Body and soul, I am marvelously made! I worship in adoration—what a creation! You know me inside and out, you know every bone in my body. You know exactly how I was made, bit by bit, how I was sculpted from nothing into something. Like an open book, you watched me grow from conception to birth. All the stages of my life were spread out before you. The days of my life all prepared before I'd even lived one day" (MSG).

Let me encourage you today. Even when you don't see God, He's working. Even when you don't feel God, He's working. He never stops working for your good. Romans 8:28 says, "And we know that all things work together for good to those who love God, to those who are the called according to His purpose" (NKJV). If life isn't good, then God isn't done. God is fighting for you. God is working for you. God is on your side. Be encouraged! You are more than a conqueror. The God that you serve is a good God, and He loves you.

1 Corinthians 13 is often referred to as the love chapter of the Bible. Let's get a clear picture of what God's love looks like. Verses 4-7 read, "Love is patient, love is kind. It does not envy, it does not boast, it is not proud. It does not dishonor others, it is not self-seeking, it is not easily angered, it keeps no record of wrongs. Love does not delight in evil but rejoices with the truth. It always protects, always trusts, always hopes, always perseveres" (NIV).

God is love. If we desire to become more like Him, we must take on His character and attributes. Friends, take some time today for self-reflection. Repeat aloud verses 4-7 and then ask yourself the following questions:

- *Love is patient. Am I willing to allow the Lord to work things out in His timing?*
- *Love is kind. Do I respond to others in a gentle way?*
- *Love does not envy. Am I envious of the success of those around me?*
- *Love does not boast. Do I boast when I DO succeed?*
- *Love is not proud. Am I a proud person? Do I struggle with pride?*
- *Love does not dishonor others. Have I shown dishonor to other people in my life?*
- *Love is not self-seeking. Do I focus solely on my needs or do I focus on helping others succeed?*
- *Love is not easily angered. Am I a peaceful person? Do I allow my emotions to escalate quickly?*
- *Love keeps no record of wrongs. Do I possess the ability to let things go or do I hold grudges that intensify over time?*
- *Love does not delight in evil but rejoices in the truth. Do I inwardly seek revenge on those who have hurt me or do I trust God to reveal the truth?*
- *Love always protects. Do I protect or expose those in my sphere of influence?*
- *Love always trusts. Do I trust God when His answers don't meet my expectations?*
- *Love always hopes. Do I believe my future is greater than my past? Am I hopeful?*
- *Love always perseveres. Is love the key factor enabling me to press on in times of difficulty?*

It was Author C.S. Lewis who said, "God loves us not because we are lovable but because He is love." If I desire love, then I must have love, and the only way to have love is to have an intimate relationship with Jesus Christ. Author and speaker Jim Rohn stated, "The major value in life is not what you get. The major value in life is what you become." The more time I spend with God, the more I become like Him. The more I read the Bible (God's love letter), the more I believe what He says about me. The more I believe what God says about me, the more I begin to love myself. I begin to understand that I am fearfully and wonderfully made (Psalm 139:14). There is a difference between the love of self and loving yourself. Worship and prayer in God's presence softens the hardened heart, heals the wounds of the past, and frees us to become who God created us to be. It was Author Tim Keller who said, "To be loved but not known is superficial. To be known and not loved is our great fear—but to be known and loved, that transforms you." God's love has transformed my life. God's love can transform your life as well. You are a child of the Most High God. Fully known. Fully accepted. Fully loved.

DAILY REFLECTION QUESTIONS

1. Do I love myself the way that Jesus loves me?
2. Do I love others the way that Jesus love others?
3. What is one thing I can do today to serve someone who has done me wrong?
4. Have I allowed myself to be transformed by God's unconditional love?
5. What does it mean to be fully known and fully loved by God?
6. What are three ways that I see God's love at work in my daily life?

I WILL BE STILL

I believe every word You've spoken
I believe You're promises are true
I believe that all my steps are ordered
In every storm You will see me through

Why do i fight these battles on my own
As if to think somehow I'm in control
So I will hold to every word you say
I know You made a way

I will be still and know that you are God
You are in control
I will be still my life is in Your hands, In Your hands
My faith will stand

I believe when call you answer
Every need You have supplied
I believe that you are always with me
Your very breath gives me life
Why do I worry I do I freak out
You said believe and never doubt
So I will hold to every word you say
I know You made a way

Standing on the rock of my salvation
Jesus You're a sure and firm foundation
I will never be afraid
I will never be afraid
Words and Music: Jared Miller

"Being still doesn't make you weak. Being still shows God that you trust Him more than you trust yourself."

I WILL BE STILL

"Sometimes God calms the storm, but sometimes
God lets the storm rage and calms His child."
-Leslie Gould

If you're like me, you don't like being still for too long. You start to go a little stir-crazy and need to move. Any kind of movement brings relief to the ever-present creature inside of you that can't be still. Although our society has become more and more sedentary, we were created for movement. We need movement in our bodies, relationships, currency, and spirit. Healthy beings move. Healthy organizations have fluid movement.

That's why I was confused by Psalm 46:10: "Be still and know that I am God" (NIV). I'm good with the "know that I am God" part, but why be still? This "being still" racked my brain and inspired me to dig deeper. According to the Hebrew translation, "Be still" literally means to let drop, abandon, sink down, withdraw. The idea is this:

Simply surrender. Ask yourself this question: Am I standing in the way of what God desires to do in my life? Whatever you are fighting, whatever you are holding onto, let it go and let it drop. By losing your life, you're actually saving it. As the phrase goes, "Let go and let God."

We often attempt to fight our battles in our own strength. This never works. It only provides a platform which we continue to build our pride upon. Surrendering to God's will doesn't mean that you lack movement, desire, or focus. Rather, every action, motive, and direction is influenced and promoted by the Holy Spirit.

I remember as a teenager hearing a story about my friend's mother who had lost all feeling in both of her legs. He told me about the times when she would work in her rose garden. The thorns would poke her repeatedly, but she never felt it. Her only indication that something was wrong was the blood she saw on her legs. Some of us are like that emotionally and spiritually. Our hearts are cold, stony, and numb from the wounds and hurts of our past. We may have thought we were healed only to find out that deep beneath the surface, toxicity was causing a slow death within our soul. This is why Ezekiel 36:26 says, "... I will take away the stony heart out of your flesh, and I will give you a heart of flesh" (KJV). A stone is cold, hard and dead. Is that how you feel? There's hope for you today. God isn't interested in giving you a temporary fix to numb the pain. No, He wants to give you an entirely new heart, vision, and outlook on life. Complete, healthy and whole—body, soul, and spirit. This is how we become "still". We die to ourselves and become alive in Christ. We "sink down" and fall into the arms of Jesus as He molds us and shapes us into who He created us to be. He created us to be more than conquerors: the head and not the tail, above and not beneath. How does this happen? Through Christ.

The book of Acts tells us that it is through Christ that we live and move and have our being. Colossians 3 says that we are "hidden" in Christ. You are not a human having a spiritual experience. Rather, you are a spirit having a human experience. Once we surrender our will to the lordship of Jesus Christ, He then takes over, guides, and influences every decision that we make. Like a person being swept away in the gentle currents of a lazy river, we too can relax, sink deep into the love of the Father knowing that we will never drown. God will carry us through every high, every low, and everything in between. There's no need to worry, stress, or doubt. If God clothes the lilies of the fields, how much more will He take care of us? All we have to do is be still and know that He is God (Psalm 46:10).

I love the hymn 'Tis So Sweet' because it beautifully describes what it means to trust in Jesus through even our darkest times. The following excerpt is written by C. Michael Hawn, professor at Southern Methodist University, explaining the origin behind the hymn.

"From her childhood, the call to missionary service was the guiding motivation for Louisa M. R. Stead (c. 1850-1917). Born in Dover, England, and converted at the age of nine, Stead came to the United States in 1871, living in Cincinnati. She attended a camp meeting in Urbana, Ohio, where she dedicated her life to missionary service. Ill health prevented her from serving initially. She married in 1875, and the couple had a daughter, Lily. Hymnologist Kenneth Osbeck describes a major turning point in the family's life:

"When the child was four years of age, the family decided one day to enjoy the sunny beach at Long Island Sound, New York. While eating their picnic lunch, they suddenly heard cries of help and spotted a drowning boy in the sea. Mr. Stead charged into the water. As often happens, however, the struggling boy pulled his rescuer under water with him, and both drowned before the terrified eyes of wife and daughter. Out of her 'why?' struggle with God during the ensuing days glowed these meaningful words from the soul of Louisa Stead:

'Tis So Sweet to trust in Jesus
Just to take Him at His word
Just to rest upon His promise
Just to know Thus saith the Lord

Jesus Jesus How I trust Him
How I prove Him Ore and ore
Jesus Jesus precious Jesus
O for grace to trust Him more

The hymn, "'Tis so sweet to trust in Jesus" was inspired by this personal tragedy."

WHEN TO BE STILL

I like to use the acronym HALT to explain the times when being still will greatly benefit you. This stands for hurt, angry, lonely, and tired. I think we can all agree that we've experienced each of these emotions at one time or another. The enemy of our souls will use these four emotions to divide us and separate us from our intended purpose in Christ. There is a time to speak up, but there is also a time to stay silent. Satan will use any hurt, any offense—anything at all in our lives—to kill, steal, and destroy us. This is why it is essential for us to release negative emotions to the Lord and allow Him to heal and restore us. As leadership expert and author John Maxwell suggests, what you don't release possesses you. "Do not take revenge, my dear friends, but leave room for God's wrath, for it is written: 'It is mine to avenge; I will repay,' says the Lord" Romans 12:19 (NIV).

Being still doesn't make you weak. Being still shows God that you trust Him more than you trust yourself. Listen to what Jesus told Peter in Luke 22:31-32: "Simon, stay on your toes. Satan has tried his best to separate all of you from me, like chaff from wheat. Simon, I've prayed for you in particular that you not give in or give out." (MSG) The enemy is always looking to divide and conquer. He wants to separate us from our purpose. Be encouraged in knowing this. Jesus is praying for you! God is fighting for you and is on your side. Don't give into your negative emotions. Minister Victor Raymond Edman said, "Never doubt in the dark what God told you in the light."

The greatest enemy we fight in life is not the devil. The greatest enemy we often fight is ourselves. There is a spiritual war that takes place in our thoughts and in our minds. Ephesians 6:12 tells us, "For we are not fighting against flesh-and-blood enemies, but against evil rulers and authorities of the unseen world, against mighty powers in this dark world, and against evil spirits in the heavenly places" (NLT). Oftentimes the battle we fight is more within ourselves than with other people. There is a peace that is released in us when we choose to surrender our battles to the Lord. We know that God is fighting for us. How incredible it is to know that God is praying for us! At Jesus' birth He is with us; at the cross He is for us. On the day of Pentecost, He is in us. The Spirit of the living God is living inside of us. Just as the body heals itself during REM sleep, so resting in the Lord fills you with peace and strength in your soul and in your spirit. As the African Proverb says, "When there is no enemy within, the enemy outside can do you no harm." The voice you trust determines the direction of your life. Allow me to encourage you today to put your total trust in Jesus. He loves you. Stand still and see the salvation of the Lord. I'll close this chapter with one of my favorite Scriptures in the Bible. Philippians 4:6-7 says, "Don't worry about anything; instead, pray about everything. Tell God what you need, and thank him for all he has done. Then you will experience God's peace, which exceeds anything we can understand. His peace will guard your hearts and minds as you live in Christ Jesus" (NLT).

DAILY REFLECTION QUESTIONS

1. When life gets hard, do I take the battle to the heavenly realm in prayer or do I try to fight my battles in my own strength?
2. Are there areas in my life where I need to be still and know that God is in control?
3. Have there been times where I have been Hurt, Angry, Lonely, or Tired? If so, have I allowed God to heal me or have I reacted negatively to these emotions?
4. Are there any offenses or grudges I have held on to that need to be released?
5. What does it mean to be "Hidden in Christ"?
6. What are some defining moments where trusting in God has brought me peace?

TAKING ME HIGHER

If all the earth would shake love would still remain
If all the ground would quake my heart could rest the same
If all the stars you made fell from the skies above
They would sing the highest praise
The wonders of Your love

Your love is taking
It's taking me
It's taking me higher

You reveal from Your view
You are making all things new
It's Your love that lifts me up
Higher and higher

"An arrow can only be shot by pulling it backward. So when life is dragging you back with difficulties, it means that it's going to launch you into something great."

TAKING ME HIGHER

*"For once you have tasted flight you will walk the earth
with your eyes turned skywards, for there you have been
and there you will long to return."*
- Leonardo da Vinci

I believe that God has put the desire in every heart to go
farther and higher in life. Ecclesiastes 3:11 tells us that, "God has
made everything beautiful for its own time. He has planted eter-
nity in the human heart, but even so, people cannot see the whole
scope of God's work from beginning to end" (NLT). God doesn't
show us the whole picture of our lives; He shows us one step at
a time, one day at a time. God knows the end from the beginning.
He is the author and the finisher of our faith. If we knew every
step ahead of us, it wouldn't require any faith on our part. Without
faith it is impossible to please God. This is a faith walk, not a sleep
walk. Psalms 37:23 says, "The Lord directs the steps of the godly.
He delights in every detail of their lives" (NLT). God is concerned

about every detail. He's concerned about the big things and the small things. The eyes of the Lord are ever on His children.

In 1 Peter 5:7, we are encouraged to "give all our worries and cares to God, for he cares about us" (NLT). Even when we make mistakes on our journey, God is faithful and true. He is a good Father. When we fall short, He doesn't beat us with a whip. Instead, He leads us with His voice. God didn't strike the worlds into existence; He spoke the worlds into existence. God is always speaking, but are we listening?

He calls his own sheep by name and leads them out. When he has brought out all his own, he goes on ahead of them, and his sheep follow him because they know his voice.
-John 10:3 (NIV)

Whether you turn to the right or to the left, your ears will hear a voice behind you, saying, "This is the way; walk in it."
-Isaiah 30:21 (NIV)

Mark out a straight path for your feet;
Stay on the safe path.
Don't get sidetracked;
Keep your feet from following evil.
-Proverbs 4:26-27 (NLT)

There are times that life can blindside us with unexpected pitfalls. It's in these times that we need to keep our eyes on Jesus and know that He will carry us through every battle and every storm. Just as Jesus called out to Peter to walk on the water, Jesus is calling out to you today.

GOD IS CALLING US FARTHER

I recently read a Facebook post that asked an interesting question: "If you could have any super power, what would it be?" The first comment posted was "a pause and rewind button." Wouldn't that be great if we could stop our lives even for only a moment to readjust, refocus, and start over? We all know that life doesn't allow us to pause and rewind. Life moves only in one direction: forward. Some of you want to go farther in your life, but you feel there are mountains in your way. By faith, look at each mountain and declare it to be removed and cast into the sea. There are seasons and times in life where you know that God is calling you into the "next" season and assignment of life. You can feel that the season you're in has shifted and that it is time to fully move into your "next." You may think you've moved on from your former season of life, but you keep looking back at what was. We all know what happened to Lot's wife when she looked back at the city from which she left; she turned to a pillar of salt. The more you look back to yesterday, the more you get stuck in yesterday—stuck in a moment.

MOVING FORWARD

All these people were still living by faith when they died. They did not receive the things promised; they only saw them and welcomed them from a distance, admitting that they were foreigners and strangers on earth. People who say such things show that they are looking for a country of their own. If they had been thinking of the country they had left, they would have had opportunity to return. Instead, they were longing for a better country—a heavenly one. Therefore God is not ashamed to be called their God, for he has prepared a city for them. - Hebrews 11:13-16 (NIV)

In Philippians 3:12-14 the apostle Paul writes, "I'm not saying that I have this all together, that I have it made. But I am well on my way, reaching out for Christ, who has so wondrously reached out for me. Friends, don't get me wrong: By no means do I count myself an expert in all of this, but I've got my eye on the goal, where God is beckoning us onward—to Jesus. I'm off and running" (MSG). Friends, let me encourage you today. In life, you have one of two choices. You either step forward into growth or back into safety. An arrow can only be shot by pulling it backward. So when life is dragging you back with difficulties, it means that it's going to launch you into something great. Keep your focus and keep aiming. Keep moving forward. The secret to change is to focus all of your energy not on fighting the old, but on building the new. Old ways won't open new doors. When was the last time you did something for the first time? God is a God of the new. God has fresh grace for you today. God is pouring out a fresh anointing in this new season you are entering. Speak this out loud by faith: "I am moving forward."

GOD IS CALLING US HIGHER

Leonardo da Vinci wrote, "For once you have tasted flight you will walk the earth with your eyes turned skywards, for there you have been and there you will long to return." I would like to add that once you have tasted flight you'll never return from whence you came. Growing up I would often hear the phrase, "Don't be so heavenly minded that you're no earthly good." I understand what was implied, but I would like to offer an alternative view. I believe the more heavenly minded we are, the more we bring heaven to earth. As believers, we can experience the atmosphere of heaven here on earth. Consider the Lord's prayer: "Thy kingdom come, Thy will be done in earth, as it is in heaven" (KJV). Jesus prayed, "Thy kingdom come," not, "Thy kingdom go." Colossians 3:1-2 says, "Since, then, you have been raised with Christ, set your hearts on things above, where Christ is, seated at the right hand of God. Set your minds on things above, not on earthly things" (NIV). What does this look like practically in our everyday lives? We forgive when people have mistreated us. When Co-workers are rude, we respond with kindness. When those around us are falling apart, we are held together by the peace of God. Our lives are a reflection of our thoughts. We think God thoughts. We live out the atmosphere of heaven.

We all are under the same sky, but we don't all have the same horizon. You see, we all came from the dirt. The place which you came from will always try to call you back. I love the illustration John Maxwell uses in his book Failing Forward:

Four monkeys were placed in a room that had a tall pole in the center. Suspended from the top of that pole was a bunch of bananas. One of the hungry monkeys started climbing the pole to get something to eat, but just as he reached out to grab a banana, he was doused with a torrent of cold water. Squealing, he scampered back down the pole and abandoned his attempt to feed himself. Each monkey made a similar attempt and each one was drenched with cold water. After making several attempts, they finally gave up. Then researchers removed one of the monkeys from the room and replaced him with a new monkey. As the newcomer began to climb the pole, the other three grabbed him and pulled him down to the ground. After trying to climb the pole several times and being dragged down by the others, he finally gave up and never attempted to climb the pole again. The researchers replaced the original monkeys, one by one, and each time a new monkey was brought in, he would be dragged down by the others before he could reach the bananas. In time, the room was filled with monkeys who had never received a cold shower. None of them would climb the pole, but not one of them knew why!

Can you relate with this story? I know I can. Have we ever stopped long enough to ask ourselves why we do what we do? Why do we settle for living on a lower level of life than God intended? Are we even aware that there is so much more for us in this life? Some people simply accept their lives when God through His Holy Spirit has given us the power to create our lives. In Psalms King David with confidence proclaims, "Indeed, with your help I can charge against an army; by my God's power I can jump over a wall" (Psalms 18:29, NET). As you read through the following Scriptures, let faith rise up in your heart. God is speaking to you in this very moment.

As you come to him, the living Stone—rejected by humans but chosen by God and precious to him— you also, like living stones, are being built into a spiritual house[a] to be a holy priesthood, offering spiritual sacrifices acceptable to God through Jesus Christ.
-1 Peter 2:4-5 (NIV)

But you are a chosen people, a royal priesthood, a holy nation, God's special possession, that you may declare the praises of him who called you out of darkness into his wonderful light.
-1 Peter 2:9 (NIV)

Arise, Jerusalem! Let your light shine for all to see. For the glory of the Lord rises to shine on you. Darkness as black as night covers all the nations of the earth, but the glory of the Lord rises and appears over you. All nations will come to your light; mighty kings will come to see your radiance. Look and see, for everyone is coming home! Your sons are coming from distant lands; your little daughters will be carried home. Your eyes will shine, and your heart will thrill with joy, for merchants from around the world will come to you.
-Isaiah 60:1-5 (NLT)

And we know that in all things God works for the good of those who love him, who have been called according to his purpose. For those God foreknew he also predestined to be conformed to the image of his Son, that he might be the firstborn among many brothers and sisters. And those he predestined, he also called; those he called, he also justified; those he justified, he also glorified. What, then, shall we say in response to these things? If God is for us, who can be against us? He who did not spare his own Son, but gave him up for us all—how will he not also, along with him, graciously give us all things? Who will bring any charge against those whom God has chosen? It is God who justifies. Who then is the one who condemns? No one. Christ Jesus who died—more than that, who was raised to life—is at the right hand of God and is also interceding for us. Who shall separate us from the love of Christ? Shall trouble or hardship or persecution or famine or nakedness or danger or sword? As it is written:

"For your sake we face death all day long;
we are considered as sheep to be slaughtered."

No, in all these things we are more than conquerors through him who loved us. For I am convinced that neither death nor life, neither angels nor demons, neither the present nor the future, nor any powers, neither height nor depth, nor anything else in all creation, will be able to separate us from the love of God that is in Christ Jesus our Lord. Roman 8:28-39 (NIV)

You can do more and be more than you ever thought possible. There are no limits when you live according to the purposes of God. Learn to say "no" to the good so you can say "yes" to the best. Stop trying to recycle what God is wanting to replace. Stop grieving over what you lost. If you needed it, you wouldn't have lost it.

"Those who regard worthless idols forsake their own mercy" (Jonah 2:8, NKJV). You can't reach for the future holding onto the past. Pastor Bill Johnson asserted, "If you look at the past long enough, you will become a monument instead of a movement." Remember that the past is a great teacher if you learn from it, but a terrible prison if you are controlled by it. We have to have an abundance mindset, not a scarcity mindset. We have to believe that our future is greater than our past. We have to believe that God has so much more in store for those who put their trust in Him.

Your miracle is not in what you have lost but in what you have gained. Focus on what God has given you. You don't have time to compare yourself to somebody else. Place all of your focus on what God has called you to do. You can choose to have a clinched fist, or you can choose to have an open hand. Remember, a clinched fist rejects but an open hand receives. James 1:17 tells us, "Every good gift and every perfect gift is from above, and comes down from the Father of lights, with whom there is no variation or shadow of turning" (NKJV). In life you have to set things right before you can see things right. Hebrews 12:1-2 describes this perfectly:

> *"Therefore we also, since we are surrounded by so great a cloud of witnesses, let us lay aside every weight, and the sin which so easily ensnares us, and let us run with endurance the race that is set before us, looking unto Jesus, the author and finisher of our faith, who for the joy that was set before Him endured the cross, despising the shame, and has sat down at the right hand of the throne of God" (NKJV).*

Jesus saw you and me. Jesus saw the past, present, and future souls that would be saved and reconciled back to Him through His sacrifice.

We were God's reason. You see, your why-power will always outlast your willpower. Jesus placed all of His focus on you and me. What was lost in the garden would be found at the cross. Our reconnection to God was so close that Jesus could taste it. The very thought that mankind would be reconciled back to God gave Jesus the strength to persevere and endure the pain of the cross. Let me encourage you today. Keep the promises of God at the forefront of your mind. Keep your eyes fixed on the joy that comes from knowing that God is leading and guiding your steps. The Bible says, "In this world you will have trouble. But take heart! I have overcome the world" (John 16:33, NIV). Sometimes God calms the storm. Sometimes He calms the child. His strength is perfected in our weakness. As author and speaker Jim Rohn said, "Don't wish that life was easier, wish that you were better. Don't wish for less problems, wish for more skills. Don't wish for less challenges, wish for more wisdom." Ask the Lord to take you higher today. He can and He will.

Circumstances try to keep us down when God's intention is for you and me to soar. The question is: What are you willing to leave behind in order to go to the next level? The higher you go the more you have to leave behind. I recently read an interesting article on eagles' ability to breathe in higher altitudes. I'd like to share it with you. The question was asked, "Do eagles have a special technique for breathing when they fly so high?" Eagles tend to use very little energy when they fly so high. Even though they can reach altitudes of over 10,000 feet, they are usually soaring to these heights, and taking long glides to cover ground, then soaring up again and repeating the process. By flying in this way, their body is really not demanding much oxygen—not any-where near as much as when they are much closer to the ground and expending considerable energy flapping their wings. Unlike any other bird, the eagle has two sets of eyelids, and one works like sunglasses. Therefore, the eagle can fly directly into the sun when a predator bird is in hot pursuit. As soon as the eagle flies into the sun, using its special sunglass eyelids, then the enemy bird is blinded by the sun and loses the eagle in the blinding light of the sun. Wow! Just like the eagle, God created you and me to soar above the clouds and glide in His presence. There is no stress in His presence. Fear and anxiety are nowhere to be found in the presence of the Lord. We are made to live and function in a spiritually higher altitude. There we find fullness of joy and peace beyond our understanding. When our eyes focus on the Son, the enemy has no chance of getting to us.

The difference between receiving and rejecting God's promises for us is an open hand. You can't have an open hand until you have an open heart. Open your heart to Him today. Believe and receive every good and perfect gift God has for you from above. Press toward the High Calling. Reach toward the High Calling. Psalms 121:1-4 says, "I will lift up my eyes to the hills—From whence comes my help? My help comes from the Lord, who made heaven and earth. He will not allow your foot to be moved; He who keeps you will not slumber. Behold, He who keeps Israel shall neither slumber nor sleep."(NKJV). God is calling us farther. God is calling us higher. I pray that you are encouraged. I pray that you would be awakened to the incomprehensible life that awaits you in Christ Jesus our Lord. As I close this chapter, my prayer for you is written in the following verses:

8-10 And so here I am, preaching and writing about things that are way over my head, the inexhaustible riches and generosity of Christ. My task is to bring out in the open and make plain what God, who created all this in the first place, has been doing in secret and behind the scenes all along. Through followers of Jesus like yourselves gathered in churches, this extraordinary plan of God is becoming known and talked about even among the angels!

14-19 My response is to get down on my knees before the Father, this magnificent Father who parcels out all heaven and earth. I ask him to strengthen you by his Spirit—not a brute strength but a glorious inner strength—that Christ will live in you as you open the door and invite him in. And I ask him that with both feet planted firmly on love, you'll be able to take in with all followers of Jesus the extravagant dimensions

of Christ's love. Reach out and experience the breadth! Test its length! Plumb the depths! Rise to the heights! Live full lives, full in the fullness of God.
-Ephesians 3:8-10/14-19, The Message

DAILY REFLECTION QUESTIONS

1. Are the words I speak taking me to a higher level or a lower level in life?
2. What dreams and visions has God given me that connect me to my purpose?
3. Does the environment I live in lift me up or drag me down?
4. Do I see the world from God's eye view or from the ground level?
5. Do I tend to hang onto my past or do I reach for the future with expectancy?
6. Identify three areas in which you desire to improve. What is your target? (It's impossible to change what you don't identify.)

LIFT UP THE NAME

Lift Up the Name
Lift Up the Name
Lift Up the Name
The Name of Jesus
No Other Name I will proclaim
No Other Name the Name of Jesus

No other name can make
Mountains tremble
Say the name and strongholds crumble
The name of Jesus
No Other name brings life into my soul
In His name I find my hope
The name of Jesus

No higher name
No greater name I know

No other name has died for my sins
In Jesus' name I've been born again
Hallelujah

No name no name is higher
No name no name is greater
In Your name we surrender all we all we are now
Lift Up The Name
Words and Music: Jared Miller

"Worship and prayer in God's presence softens the hardened heart, heals the wounds of the past, and frees us to become who God created us to be."

LIFT UP THE NAME

"You were created to live in God's presence. Life anywhere else is a distorted, dissatisfying imitation."
-Myles Munroe

We were created for worship. According to Merriam-Webster, worship means "to regard with great or extravagant respect, honor, or devotion. Everyone worships something or someone. What do we value most in life? Who or what receives our highest level of respect, honor, and devotion? The answer is found in what we worship. Whatever gets our full energy, time, and attention is a direct reflection of its worth and value in our lives. Anything we worship other than God is considered an idol. It's "the little foxes, that spoil the vines" (Song of Solomon 2:15, KJV). It's the cares of this world that tend to zap our energy, time, and attention off of its original purpose. Friends, let's be intentional with who or what gets the best of us. God deserves our best. He gave His best for us. When we prioritize God first in our lives, everything else falls into place as it should. Set aside some time today for self-reflection.

What do you idolize? What are you holding onto that God is asking you to let go of? What is lifted up before you in your own eyes? Do you tend to be more self-serving or more prone to serving others? Something and someone will always be at the forefront of your thoughts and emotions. The voice you give your greatest attention to determines the direction of your life. What influences you most receives your greatest focus.

CREATED TO WORSHIP

Worship simply put is the outward physical expression of an inward transformation. Pastor and gospel recording artist William McDowell said, "Our worship to God is directly connected to our revelation of who God is." Luke 19:37-40 describes the natural inclination of creation expressing worship: "Then, as He was now drawing near the descent of the Mount of Olives, the whole multitude of the disciples began to rejoice and praise God with a loud voice for all the mighty works they had seen, saying: 'Blessed is the King who comes in the name of the Lord! Peace in heaven and glory in the highest!' And some of the Pharisees called to Him from the crowd, 'Teacher, rebuke Your disciples.' But He answered and said to them, 'I tell you that if these should keep silent, the stones would immediately cry out'" (NKJV).

Creation was made to worship. Our God is worthy of worship. He will receive worship and honor either from humanity or a stone. Either way, God will be worshiped. Even creation understands its natural response in the presence of glory. I pray that we understand this as well. The late Myles Munroe beautifully penned,

"You were created to live in God's presence. Life anywhere else is a distorted, dissatisfying imitation."

THE VALUE OF A NAME

"A good name is to be chosen rather than great riches, Loving favor rather than silver and gold" (Proverbs 22:1, KJV). As someone who pastors and works with people every day, I can tell you with full confidence that we all love being called by name. We appreciate it even more when our names are pronounced correctly. Isn't it true that we feel more valued and respected when someone remembers our name? We feel more engaged in a conversation when someone uses our name. "A person's name is to him or her the sweetest and most important sound in any language," writes Dale Carnegie in his classic book How to Win Friends and Influence People.

The truth is that names are a part of every culture and that they are of enormous importance both to the people who receive names and to the ones that give them. Regardless of when, why, or how often it happens, the giving and receiving of a name is an event of major importance. Your name is of the utmost importance. Your name has the history of your ancestry and family lineage. Your name gives you identity and a sense of belonging. When a woman gets married, she takes on her husband's last name. Her identity changes when she becomes one with her husband. The same is true in our relationship with Christ. The moment we receive the revelation of who God is and what He has done for us is the moment we surrender our lives to Him. Our natural response to our Creator is to take on His nature. We take on His Name. We become one. Colossians 3:1-4 says, "Since you have been raised to new life with Christ, set your sights on the realities of heaven, where Christ sits in the place of honor at God's right hand. Think about the things of heaven, not the things of earth. For you died to this life, and your real life is hidden with Christ in God. And when

Christ, who is your life, is revealed to the whole world, you will share in all his glory" (NLT). As sons and daughters of the Most High God, we have access to everything our Father has. Being "hidden in Christ" signifies that our life is no longer our own but belongs completely to God. We now live and operate from His character and attitude.

You must have the same attitude that Christ Jesus had. Though he was God, he did not think of equality with God as something to cling to. Instead, he gave up his divine privileges he took the humble position of a slave and was born as a human being. When he appeared in human form, he humbled himself in obedience to God and died a criminal's death on a cross. Therefore, God elevated him to the place of highest honor and gave him the name above all other names, that at the name of Jesus every knee should bow, in heaven and on earth and under the earth, and every tongue declare that Jesus Christ is Lord, to the glory of God the Father.
Philippians 2:5-11 (NLT)

It was Mark Batterson who said, "You cannot build God's reputation if you aren't willing to risk yours." What happens when God is lifted up in your life? You see things from God's perspective, because what you behold you become. Your outlook on life changes. Your worldview shifts from one of an earthly realm to that of a heavenly realm. You love what God loves, and you reject anything contrary to the nature of Heaven. You begin to function and live out from the environment that you live in. When you lift God up, He lifts you up. Ephesians 2:6 says that we are to be seated with Jesus in heavenly places. Just as eagles do not get entangled with the affairs of the ground, so we as children of God soar above the clouds of life and rest in the Son. As I stated earlier, you are not a human having a spiritual experience. You are a spirit having a human experience. I don't know about you, but I want my head in the clouds. I want to be so awestruck and so captivated by God's glory and love until that's all I see and all I know. The presence of God in the believer's life heightens an awareness of His greatness. We are overcome with gratitude and thanksgiving. We are possessed with the peace of God. The Bible says our words come from the overflow of our hearts (Luke 6:45). The overflow is what we give to those around us every day.

John 3:16-17 says, "For God so loved the world that he gave his one and only Son, that whoever believes in him shall not perish but have eternal life. For God did not send his Son into the world to condemn the world, but to save the world through him" (NIV). God is love, and God loves people. We should unconditionally give others the same love God has shown to us. We should unconditionally show the same grace to others that God has shown to us. When you love people, you are demonstrating the heart of God. The hands and feet of Jesus encourage, love, and bless people. They take people to a higher place than they could ever go on their own. From that higher place, we view life from a heavenly perspective. We begin to manifest the glory of God in our everyday lives.

We are called to live a life of worship. We are called to make disciples of all nations. We have a purpose and a mandate to bring heaven to earth. Our ambition is not one of selfish desires but rather one of building the kingdom of God. Godly ambition says, "I only want something at the service of others, not at the expense of others." There's nothing wrong with passion, work ethic, and ambition. Just make sure that when you're climbing the ladder of success that you take someone with you. Some people are climbers, but they're not connecters. Some people are leaners when they should be lifters.

The church will see revival when we spend less time correcting people and spend more time connecting with them. In every relationship, nothing is more important than loving people. You never know the impact that you have on another person. Love them, pray for them, serve them, pour into them, build them up, take them to a higher level as Christ has taken you to a higher level. We live in a world filled with negativity and division. We as believers have the opportunity to show the love of God to a hurting world in desperate need to see the living Jesus at work in our daily lives. He gives us opportunities to serve, give and love people. Remember, opportunities are never lost, they are simply found by someone else—someone whose head is lifted and whose eyes are on the Lord.

3 CHARACTERISTICS OF LIFTERS

1. THEY SHOW GENUINE APPRECIATION

Philippians 1:3 says, "I thank my God upon every remembrance of you" (NKJV). Paul is thanking God anytime he thinks about the people of Philippi and is filled with appreciation for them. John 1:1 says, "In the beginning was the Word, and the Word was with God, and the Word was God" (NIV). Everything begins with a thought. In the Greek, Word in this scripture is translated as thought. With that in mind, lets re-read John 1:1 this way: "In the beginning was the Word [Thought] and the Word [Thought] was with God and the Word [Thought] was God." God's thoughts toward me are good and not evil. Before I was born God knew me. No two thumbprints are alike. "I am fearfully and wonderfully made" (Psalm 139:14, NIV). The moment I believe that and receive that, I begin to live that out. The feeling that God values me and appreciates me causes me in return to do the same for others. I want to think like God thinks. I want to appreciate people the way that God does. How do we accomplish this?

TRADE EXPECTATION FOR APPRECIATION

James Gray serves on our usher team at New Covenant Church in Humble, Texas, where I have had the honor of pastoring our worship ministry and leading the congregation in song and worship for thirteen years. Anyone who has the privilege of knowing James will tell you that one major quality stands out above the rest: James is an encourager. He is not like some people who give you lip service just to make you feel good. No, he is the real deal. Without fail, after every service James comes up to me and says, "Great job with the music. You guys sound better and better every week". I realize that might sound like a generic thing to say, but here's the catch: what you don't know is that James is in his sixties and if he had it his way, we would sing the old gospel hymn "I'll Fly Away" every Sunday. I mean every Sunday. This is a hard-working family man hearing our worship team lead the church in a diversity of musical styles including but not limited to: gospel, CCM (Contemporary Christian Music), hymns, pop, and gospel choir selections. What was not mentioned? Southern gospel music—which I love, by the way. This is a man who genuinely encourages our worship team even though we are not singing and playing his "stylistic preference" of worship music. I feel appreciated by James every time the doors of the church are open. Friends, when was the last time you encouraged someone like that? It is an incredible feeling.

Bless the Lord, O my soul;
And all that is within me, bless His holy name!
Bless the Lord, O my soul,
And forget not all His benefits:
Who forgives all your iniquities,
Who heals all your diseases,
Who redeems your life from destruction,
Who crowns you with lovingkindness and tender mercies,
Who satisfies your mouth with good things,
So that your youth is renewed like the eagle's.
Psalm 103: 1-5, (NKJV)

Appreciation takes you high above so you can soar like an eagle. Where your focus goes your energy flows. Focus on showing true appreciation and the love of God to all people, even the people who think and live differently than you do.

2. THEY HONOR ALL PEOPLE

There are many definitions of honor, but allow me to show you one that really sticks out to me. Honor is the ability to discern difference instead of weakness. Honor is directly related to your level of perception of people. How do you view people? Do you choose to see divine difference or weakness in others? Choose to honor people based on their best moments, not their worst moments. We must all make a choice to see others as God sees them. This takes discipline and focus on our part. We must be intentional about honoring all people as Jesus did. 1 Peter 2:17 instructs us to honor all people. When you show honor to others, you are showing honor to God. What you do for others, God will do for you. Interestingly in the King James Version of the Bible, the word leader is mentioned six times, however, the word servant is mentioned 900 times. Jesus said, "Whatever you did for one of the least of these brothers and sisters of mine, you did for me" (Matthew 25:40, NIV). When you help those who cannot help themselves, it captivates the heart of God.

In the Old Testament we see where David showed King Saul honor even the Saul was trying to kill him. The Scriptures record David declaring, "Don't destroy him! No one can do any harm to the Lord's anointed king and not be guilty" (1 Samuel 26:9, NIRV). There are times in your life when people will mistreat you. Let the Lord fight those battles for you. You show honor to God when you trust Him to fight for you. By releasing your situations into His hands, you are showing God that you trust Him and know that He can handle your battles much better than you can. On the cross Jesus was fully God and fully man, yet while He was being crucified, Jesus looked at the Roman soldiers and said, "Father, forgive them, for they know not what they do" Luke 23:34 (ESV). In the most vulnerable and humbling moment of Jesus's life, He still showed honor to the people and asked His Father to forgive them. Wow! Let us follow Jesus's example and show honor to all people.

3. THEY CELEBRATE THE GOODNESS OF GOD

What do we celebrate? We celebrate what we value the most. How do we celebrate the goodness of God? Through worship! Our worship expresses our greatest value and worth is found in Jesus Christ. Thanksgiving is the prerequisite to praise and worship. Psalm 118:24 declares, "This is the day that the Lord has made; let us rejoice and be glad in it" (ESV). Psalm 100:4 proclaims, "Enter his gates with thanksgiving and his courts with praise; give thanks to him and praise his name" (NIV). Take a look at what Philippians 4:4-5 from The Message Bible says about celebrating God's goodness: "Celebrate God all day, every day. I mean, revel in him! Make it as clear as you can to all you meet that you're on their side, working with them and not against them. Help them see that the Master is about to arrive. He could show up any minute!" In Psalm 34:1-3 King David declares, "I will bless the Lord at all times; his praise shall continually be in my mouth. My soul shall make its boast in the Lord; the humble shall hear thereof, and be glad. O magnify the Lord with me, and let us exalt his name together" (KJV). Friends, there are few things in life I can think of that are better than when we gather together to praise and worship our God.

Let's look at the definition of praise. Merriam-Webster defines praise as a verb that means to "express warm approval or admiration of." It can also be used as a noun, meaning "the expression of approval or admiration for someone or something." Sitting in silence during worship is not praising God; that's called meditation. Meditation is beneficial and necessary in the life the believer. However, when it comes to praise, a shout rises from within and bursts forth in an expression of gratitude and thanksgiving. Remember, everything begins with a thought. Thoughts become words. Words create decisions. Decisions turn into actions. Actions develop into habits. Habits form our character. Character keeps us on the road to our divine destiny. God's plan and purpose for our lives began with a thought. I love what the apostle Paul wrote in Philippians 4:8: "Finally, brothers and sisters, whatever is true, whatever is noble, whatever is right, whatever is pure, whatever is lovely, whatever is admirable—if anything is excellent or praiseworthy—think about such things" (NIV).

Think on the goodness of God. If life isn't good for you right now, just remember that God isn't finished yet. In the end, everything is going to be alright. Romans 8:28 says, "And we know that all things work together for good to those who love God, to those who are the called according to His purpose" (NKJV). You see, worship is all about Jesus. Jesus isn't just our Savior, He is our Lord. He reigns over all creation. Our lives are surrendered to His purposes, not our purposes. When we get that twisted, we become frustrated and impatient wondering why life isn't happening at the speed or at the way we thought it should go. All things work together for His purposes. It's by Him that "we live and move and have our being" (Acts 17:28, NIV). Our very lives are being held together by the God of the universe. He is worthy of all the praise and all the glory. The more I think about this reality, the more I desire to spend time in His presence and lift Him up. His presence moves me. His presence changes me. It was James Allen who stated, "You cannot travel within and stand still without." There's a song written by James Huey titled "When I Think About the Lord." It reminds me of all the wonderful things God has done in my life. It keeps me humble and hungry for more of Him. I pray that the following lyrics bless you as much as they bless me:

When I think about the Lord,
How He saved me, how He raised me,
How He filled me with the Holy Ghost.
How He healed me, to the uttermost.
When I think about the Lord,
How He picked me up and turned me around,
How he placed my feet on solid ground
It makes me wanna shout,

Hallelujah!
Thank you Jesus!
Lord, You're worthy, of all the glory, and all the honor,
And all the praise.

DAILY REFLECTION QUESTIONS

1. Is my greatest worth and value found in Jesus?
2. Do I daily express my worship and gratitude to the Lord?
3. In my life, am I building God's kingdom or my own reputation?
4. Do I show genuine appreciation to other people?
5. Do I honor all people?
6. Do I daily remind myself of the goodness of God?

FAITHFUL

Even when my eyes can't see
In my spirit I believe
That Your word is ever true
You work all things for my good

You are faithful
Jesus I believe that you are able
able to complete the work
You started in me
I will worship
Lift my hands and sing for You are worthy
Worthy of all praise and all the glory
Jesus You are faithful

Even when my strength is gone
In my weakness You are strong
If I am faithless still You are faithful
Lord You remain the same

The gates not hell will not prevail
against Your promise
The gates of hell will not prevail
You are God and Lord of all
We declare
Your word will never fail
Words and Music: Jared Miller

"God sees the end from the beginning; He is faithful to complete what He started in you."

FAITHFUL

God is not a man, that He should lie, Nor a son of man,
that He should repent. Has He said, and will He not do it?
Or has He spoken, and will He not make it good?
- Numbers 23:19, NASB

It's easy to be a critic. It take zero faith, zero optimism. Anyone can criticize and tear someone down. However, it takes faith and trust in God to maintain a right spirit and proper perspective. We live in a world filled with doubters, haters, and mockers, but I want to be a believer. I desire to increase my faith. I want to trust God more today than I did yesterday. Hebrews 11:6 tells us, "But without faith it is impossible to please Him, for he who comes to God must believe that He is, and that He is a rewarder of those who diligently seek Him" (NKJV). Proverbs 3:5-6 instructs us to "Trust in the Lord with all your heart, and lean not on your own understanding; In all your ways acknowledge Him, and He shall direct your paths" (NKJV).

Faith is trusting God on the front-end with what will only be revealed on the back-end. I desire to have child-like faith that in its purest form fully obeys and trusts the Lord. It's important to remember that what you force is fear-based. What you allow is faith-based. Your miracle is on the other side of your obedience. Obedience is based on trust. When you trust God, His provision always prevails. Even in our moments of testing, our God is faithful. I can't think of a better portion of Scripture describing God testing someone's faith more than Genesis 22:1-18:

> Some time later, God tested Abraham's faith.
> "Abraham!" God called.
> "Yes," he replied. "Here I am."
> "Take your son, your only son—yes, Isaac, whom you love so much—and go to the land of Moriah. Go and sacrifice him as a burnt offering on one of the
> mountains, which I will show you."

> The next morning Abraham got up early. He saddled his donkey and took two of his servants with him, along with his son, Isaac. Then he chopped wood for a fire for a burnt offering and set out for the place God had told him about. On the third day of their journey, Abraham looked up and saw the place in the distance. "Stay here with the donkey," Abraham told the servants. "The boy and I will travel a little farther. We will worship there, and then we will come right back."

> So Abraham placed the wood for the burnt offering on Isaac's shoulders, while he himself carried the fire and the knife. As the two of them walked on together, Isaac turned to Abraham and said,
> "Father?"

"Yes, my son?" Abraham replied.

"We have the fire and the wood," the boy said, "but where is the sheep for the burnt offering?"

"God will provide a sheep for the burnt offering, my son," Abraham answered.

And they both walked on together.

When they arrived at the place where God had told him to go, Abraham built an altar and arranged the wood on it. Then he tied his son, Isaac, and laid him on the altar on top of the wood. And Abraham picked up the knife to kill his son as a sacrifice. At that moment the angel of the Lord called to him from heaven,

"Abraham! Abraham!"

"Yes," Abraham replied. "Here I am!"

"Don't lay a hand on the boy!" the angel said. "Do not hurt him in any way, for now I know that you truly fear God. You have not withheld from me even your son, your only son."

Then Abraham looked up and saw a ram caught by its horns in a thicket. So he took the ram and sacrificed it as a burnt offering in place of his son. Abraham named the place Yahweh-Yireh (which means "the Lord will provide"). To this day, people still use that name as a proverb: "On the mountain of the Lord it will be provided."

Then the angel of the Lord called again to Abraham from heaven. "This is what the Lord says: Because you have obeyed me and have not withheld even your son, your only son, I swear by my own name that I will certainly bless you. I will multiply your descendants beyond number, like the stars in the sky and the sand on the seashore. Your descendants will conquer the cities of their enemies. And through your descendants all the nations of the earth will be blessed—all because you have obeyed me" (NLT).

When you surrender to God what is most precious to you, God gives back so much more. "A good measure, pressed down, shaken together and running over" (Luke 6:38, NIV). God will always provide a ram in the bush. God can give you a coin from a fish's mouth (Matthew 17:24-27). He is a Way-Maker, a Miracle Worker, a Promise Keeper. You might be saying, "My life doesn't have much to show for itself." Give it to God. Give God your 5 loaves and 2 fish. With you, 5 loaves plus 2 fish equals 7. With God, 5 loaves plus 2 fish equals 5000. Trust God with your current season of life. Trust God with your future. Trust God with your finances. Trust God with your spouse. Trust God with your family. Trust God with your church. Trust God with your relationships. Trust God with your life. I obey because I believe God is faithful, and "He is a rewarder of those who diligently seek Him" (Hebrews 11:6, NKJV).

WE ALL HAVE PROBLEMS

Let's look at the patriarchs of our faith and how God used them in spite of their problems.

- Abraham lied.
- Sarah laughed at God's promises.
- Moses stuttered.
- David's armor didn't fit.
- John Mark was rejected by Paul.
- Timothy had ulcers.
- Hosea's wife was a prostitute.
- Amos' only training was in the school of fig-tree pruning.
- Jacob was a liar.
- David had an affair.
- Solomon was too rich.
- Jesus was too poor.

- Abraham was too old.
- David was too young.
- Peter was afraid of death.
- Lazarus was dead.
- John was self-righteous.
- Naomi was a widow.
- Paul was a murderer. So was Moses.
- Jonah ran from God.
- Miriam was a gossip.
- Gideon and Thomas both doubted.
- Jeremiah was depressed and suicidal.
- Elijah was burned out.
- John the Baptist was a loudmouth.
- Martha was a worry-wort.
- Mary may have been lazy.
- Samson had long hair.
- Noah got drunk.
- Did I mention Moses had a short fuse?
- So did Peter, Paul, and lots of other people.

God can take our problems and turn them into possibilities if we trust His process for our lives. Pastor Bill Johnson said, "Faith doesn't deny a problem's existence. It denies a problem its place of influence." If we surrender to the process of trusting and obeying God, we will ultimately find HIs purpose for our lives. God sees the end from the beginning. He is in control. He is faithful to complete what He started in you.

As I close the final chapter of this book, I'd like to leave you with these words from S.M. Lockridge:

YOU CAN TRUST HIM

"He is the one who made us, it is He who made us and not we ourselves. The heavens declare the glory of God and the Firmament shows His handiwork. No means of measurement can define His limitless love and no far seeing telescope can bring into visibility the coastline of His shoreless supply. I'm telling you today you can trust Him.

No barrier can hinder Him from pouring out His blessings. He is enduringly strong and entirely secure. He is eternally steadfast. He is immortally graceful. He is imperially powerful. He is impartially merciful. He is the greatest phenomenon that has ever crossed the horizon of this world. He is God's son, the sinner's savior. He is the center piece of civilization. I am trying to tell you, church, you can trust Him.

He does not have to call for help, and you cannot confuse Him. He doesn't need you and He doesn't need me. He stands alone in solitude of Himself. He's august and He's unique. He's unparalleled, He's unprecedented, He is supreme, He is preeminent, He is the loftiest idea in literature. He is the highest personality in philosophy. He is the supreme problem of higher criticism. He is the fundamental doctrine of true theology. He is the cardinal necessity of a spiritual religion. He is the miracle of the age. He is the superlative of everything good that you can call Him. I'm trying to tell you, church, that you can trust Him.

He can satisfy all your needs, He can do it simultaneously. He supplies strength to the weak. He's available for the tempted and the tried. He sympathizes and He sees. He guards and He guides. He heals the sick, He cleanses lepers, He forgives sinners, He discharges debtors. He delivers the captives, He defends the feeble, He blesses the young. He regards the aged, He rewards the diligent, He beautifies the meek. I'm trying to tell you, church, you can trust Him.

He's the key to knowledge, He's the well spring of wisdom. He's the doorway of deliverance, He's the pathway of peace. He's the roadway of righteousness. He is the highway of holiness. He is the gateway of glory. You can trust Him.

He is the master of the mighty, He is the captain of the conquerors, the head of Heroes. He is the leader of legislators. He is the overseer of the overcomers. He is the governor of the governors. He is the prince of princes. He is the king of kings. He is the Lord of Lords. You can trust Him.

His office is manifold. His promise is sure. His life is matchless. His goodness is limitless. His mercy is everlasting. His love never changes. His word is enough. His grace is sufficient. His reign is righteous. His yoke is easy. His burden is light. I wish I could describe Him to you.

He is indescribable because He is incomprehensible. He is irresistible because He is invincible.

You can't get Him off your hands. You can't get Him off your mind. You can't outlive Him, and you can't live without Him. Pilate couldn't stand it when he found out he couldn't stop Him and Pilate couldn't find any fault in Him. The witnesses couldn't get their testimonies to agree. Herod couldn't kill Him, death couldn't handle Him and thank God the grave couldn't hold Him. There was nobody before Him, there will be nobody after Him. He has no predecessor. He'll have no successor. You can't impeach Him, and He's not going to resign. You can trust Him."

To love God is to know God. To know God is to trust God. To trust God is to obey God. God is Faithful.

DAILY REFLECTION QUESTIONS

1. Do I fully trust God when life brings disappointment?
2. Do I see problems as obstacles or opportunities to increase my faith?
3. What are three areas in my life where God has proven to be a provider?
4. In my daily life, do I walk by faith or do I walk by sight?
5. Where has God proved faithful in spite of my times of doubting Him?
6. Am I willing to say "no" to the good so I can say "yes" to the best God has for me?

CONCLUSION

I pray that this book has resonated with you and encouraged you to know God in a greater capacity than ever before. Make it a habit every day to speak the promises of God over your life. You are loved by the God of the universe. God is crazy about you, and His love will never stop chasing you down. His plan and purpose is to take your faith to a higher dimension where you are, as the Scriptures say, "seated... with Jesus in the heavenly places" (Ephesians 2:6, ESV).

When we lift up His Name and worship Him, His presence is made manifest in our lives. It's in these moments that we can be still and know that He is God. We might not know what the future holds, but we know who holds the future. Our God is with us and our God is for us. Our God is faithful. I would love to hear from you how this book has connected with you. Until then, I'd like to leave you with a blessing from Numbers 6:24-26:

The Lord bless you
and keep you;
the Lord make his face shine on you
and be gracious to you;
the Lord turn his face toward you
and give you peace (NIV).

www.ingramcontent.com/pod-product-compliance
Lightning Source LLC
LaVergne TN
LVHW051153080426
835508LV00021B/2599